Tredegar Park, Newport. The gates here were made by the Bristol smith William Edney in 1713-18 for £550. They are a classic composition standing in front of the house, enclosing a forecourt.

Wrought Iron

Richard Hayman

Shire Publications

Contents

Cover photographs: *(Left upper) The overthrow of the eighteenth-century gates at Penshurst Place, Kent. The gates were made for Wingerworth Hall in Derbyshire by Robert Bakewell but were subsequently moved to Penshurst. (Left lower) Thirteenth-century ironwork on the door of Uffington church, Oxfordshire. (Right) The White Gates at Leeswood Hall, Flintshire, made by Robert Davies for Sir George Wynne in 1726.*

ACKNOWLEDGEMENTS

All photographs are by the author except those of the tomb of Queen Eleanor at Westminster Abbey (page 11), which is from the National Monuments Record, and of the tomb of Edward IV (page 14, top), which is reproduced by permission of the Dean and Canons of Windsor. The catalogue of the 1862 International Exhibition was kindly made available to me for copying by John Powell, librarian of the Ironbridge Gorge Museum Trust.

British Library Cataloguing in Publication Data: Hayman, Richard. Wrought iron. – (Shire album; 350) 1. Wrought-iron – Great Britain – History 2. Wrought-iron – Great Britain – Guidebooks I. Title 669.1'414'0941 ISBN 0 7478 0441 9.

Published in 2000 by Shire Publications Ltd, Cromwell House, Church Street, Princes Risborough, Buckinghamshire HP27 9AA, UK. (Website: www.shirebooks.co.uk)

Copyright © 2000 by Richard Hayman. First published 2000. Shire Album 350. ISBN 0 7478 0441 9.

Richard Hayman is hereby identified as the author of this work in accordance with Section 77 of the Copyright, Designs and Patents Act 1988.

Printed in Great Britain by CIT Printing Services Ltd, Press Buildings, Merlins Bridge, Haverfordwest, Pembrokeshire SA61 1XF.

Introduction

Wrought iron has been used as a decorative element in architecture for over a thousand years. It is a versatile metal, capable of being applied to flat surfaces like doors or used for freestanding structures like gates and railings. If treated properly it is robust and durable, while it provides a medium for both strength and delicacy in form and decoration.

Wrought iron is the purest form of iron. Like mild steel, which has replaced it, wrought iron is malleable and can be welded, whereas cast iron, which has a 3–4 per cent carbon content and can be poured into moulds, is brittle when cold. Medieval smiths were supplied with iron from small furnaces known as bloomeries. From the sixteenth century these were gradually superseded by blast furnaces, from where pig iron had to be sent to forges known as fineries and chaferies for a further refining stage in order to produce malleable bars that could be worked up at smithies.

Melbourne Hall, Derbyshire, looking up through the arbour designed and built by Robert Bakewell, 1707–11.

The smith, from a medieval German book of trades. The smith heated the iron by placing it in a charcoal-fuelled hearth, which can be seen in the background, then forged it manually on an anvil.

Ironwork was forged using techniques and equipment that have remained in use since the tenth century. A hearth is needed to heat the iron, a water tank to cool it, and a hammer and an anvil to work it. The anvil is the block for hammering and generally has a horned end and a blunt end (or heel). Blacksmiths worked from iron rods or bars which were heated and hammered into shape; the most natural shape was the scroll, the standard motif in decorative wrought iron. Simple dies, also known as *swages*, were used to hammer out patterns, a technique known as *chasing* or *jagging*, and which is still used. Other techniques, such as die stamping, carving and repoussé work, were major innovations in their own right and will be described in more detail below. From the 1860s mild steel began to supersede wrought iron, which was no longer produced to any significant extent in the twentieth century.

Scrollwork in the gates to the chantry chapel at Farleigh Hungerford Castle, Somerset, made in 1465–70 for the tomb of Sir Thomas Hungerford. The scroll is the characteristic motif of decorative ironwork.

4

Doors and chests

Wrought iron was applied to medieval doors and wooden chests to decorate and reinforce them. On doors, decorative ironwork developed from the need to hang the door on hinges and as a means of binding together the wooden battens (vertical planks). Although no Anglo-Saxon ironwork has survived *in situ*, the general design of decorative ironwork in this period has been revealed from manuscript illustrations and was formed of horizontal bars with elaborate scrollwork. A similar motif survived into the Norman period and can be seen on a number of doors, such as those at Edstaston, Worfield and Morville (Shropshire) and Old Woking (Surrey), as a horizontal bar ornamented with friezes of horseshoe-shaped scrolls.

Beginning in the period when Norman architecture established itself in Britain, from 1066 until the end of the twelfth century, decorative ironwork was based upon

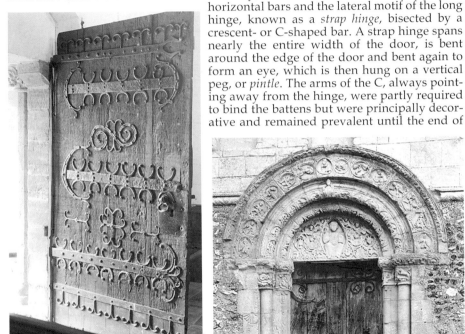

horizontal bars and the lateral motif of the long hinge, known as a *strap hinge*, bisected by a crescent- or C-shaped bar. A strap hinge spans nearly the entire width of the door, is bent around the edge of the door and bent again to form an eye, which is then hung on a vertical peg, or *pintle*. The arms of the C, always pointing away from the hinge, were partly required to bind the battens but were principally decorative and remained prevalent until the end of

Above: *Morville, Shropshire. A twelfth-century door with Saxon-style ironwork, consisting of horizontal bars and strap hinges with horseshoe scrolls.*

Right: *The Norman doorway at Barfreston, Kent. Although the ironwork on the door is later, the C-scrolls are a Norman motif and the doorway with its carved tympanum illustrates the architectural setting of twelfth-century ironwork.*

Stillingfleet, North Yorkshire. The surviving ironwork on the door has zoomorphic motifs but is otherwise religious in character, with a scrolled cross, and Adam and Eve and the Tree of Knowledge in the top left corner.

the thirteenth century.

The most elaborate Norman doors were further embellished with pictorial schemes, five of which have survived in a fragmentary form: at Stillingfleet (North Yorkshire), Staplehurst (Kent), Worfield (Shropshire), Runhall (Norfolk) and Old Woking (Surrey). In each case the pictorial scheme is concentrated at the top of the door and fulfils the practical need to span the surface of the door with reinforcing ironwork, but whether any of them represents a single integrated composition is doubtful. The ironwork can be seen as an element of design in the same way that Norman doorways had elaborate columns and arches, with perhaps a carved image on the semi-circular tympanum framed by the arch, but with no single theme.

Pictorial doors have often been interpreted as displaying Viking influence, but this is far from certain. For example, chief among the representational elements on the Stillingfleet door is a masted ship with a zoomorphic bow and a steering oar, of a kind that looks Viking but is known also from the Bayeux Tapestry and remained in use until the thirteenth century. Crosses with scrolled arms are found here and are a common feature of Norman doors, the shape of the cross being readily suited to forging in iron, irrespective of its religious significance. Trees are also found on other contemporary doors, such as at Edstaston (Shropshire), possibly representing the Tree of Life, a common symbol often seen in the tympana of Norman doorways.

The development of ironwork from the twelfth to the fourteenth centuries was to follow the general trend in architecture and decoration embodied in the Gothic style. Norman architecture tended to produce flat surfaces upon which decoration

Staplehurst, Kent. The Norman door retains zoomorphic designs, a boat and fish, but they are not grouped into a readily intelligible composition.

The pictorial Norman door at Worfield, Shropshire, now moved inside the church. Apart from fish and birds, the ironwork displays characteristic Norman features such as C-scrolls, crosses and bars with horse-shoe scrolls.

could be applied as a feature in its own right. The pictorial doors are the perfect demonstration of this. However, the spirit of Gothic architecture was more abstract and linear, while decoration was subordinated to structure in a far more disciplined manner. The C-hinge that bisected the strap hinge slowly went out of favour. Instead, strap hinges sprouted foliage in stylised scrolls, forming swirling arabesques covering the entire surface of the door, and yet always flowing from the hinge, the basic structural element. Some of the best doors of the late thirteenth century, as at Uffington (Oxfordshire), embody a transitional phase where the two motifs are combined.

The final artistic development in the ironwork of medieval doors was to reduce the visual dominance of the hinge in favour of an all-over pattern with a vertical instead of a horizontal axis. All-over patterns had been used in the twelfth century,

Abbey Dore, Herefordshire. A fourteenth-century strap hinge whose flowing style follows the direction of the hinge like the branches of a tree.

7

Above left: *The florid strap hinges on the door at Meare, Somerset, are typical of the flowing forms of fourteenth-century architecture.*

Above right: *Dartmouth, Devon. The door is probably fifteenth-century and has strap hinges conceived as two heraldic leopards. Both hinges are bisected by the branch of a tree with stylised foliage and shallow roots, probably representing the Tree of Life and a particularly successful way to introduce iron across the entire surface area. Leopards were the arms of the Plantagenet kings of England, who reigned between 1154 and 1485.*

as at Durham Cathedral. An intermediate form is the door at Dartmouth (Devon), where a tree provides a vertical axis to the composition but is bisected by strap hinges in the form of heraldic leopards. Fully developed examples of the style, like the doors at York Minster and St George's Chapel in Windsor Castle (Berkshire), show the influence of the earliest freestanding iron screens.

Smiths were evidently important craftsmen in the early Middle Ages, but not until the latter half of the thirteenth century do any of their names become known. The most famous is Thomas of Leighton (probably Leighton Buzzard), who was paid £12 in 1294–5 for making and erecting a screen at Westminster Abbey, London. Thomas is also well known as a master of the technique of die stamping. This should not be confused with the simpler swages used for chasing the metal surface. A *die*

The church at Eaton Bray, Bedfordshire, is one of the most complete English parish churches of the thirteenth century. Among its special features is the fine ironwork, an early example of the die-stamping technique. The scrolls cover the whole area of the door.

was a hardened steel stamp cut with a design, usually small rosettes or leaves. It was hammered on to heated bars and was employed to cover the weld of two bars or to terminate the tendrils of foliage designs. Sometimes the bar was hammered to produce a continuous indented profile.

Although thirteenth-century smiths all used a similar repertoire of stamps, they were responsible for making their own dies. Thomas of Leighton's characteristic designs used at Westminster Abbey have been found on the church doors at Turvey

and Leighton Buzzard (Bedfordshire). In one of the earliest examples of stamped work, made c.1240 for a door at St George's Chapel in Windsor Castle, a smith stamped his name 'Gilbertus'. The technique was also used throughout the fourteenth century and is commonly seen on doors, chests and cupboards, like the aumbry doors at Chester Cathedral and a wooden chest at Malpas (Cheshire), probably by the same craftsman.

The chest at Malpas, Cheshire. The iron adds strength to the chest and is die-stamped by a smith who was probably responsible for work at Chester Cathedral.

Above left: *Baltonsborough, Somerset. A finely wrought fifteenth-century door handle with crosses incised into the plate.*

Above right: *Stogumber, Somerset. A sixteenth-century door handle with an incised, twisted effect used for the ring handle and the border around the plate.*

During the Middle Ages wooden chests were used by parishes to hold valuable items like parish records and other documents. They were constructed either by gouging out a piece of tree trunk and providing a hinged lid, or by means of horizontal oak planks. The latter were normally reinforced with decorative straps similar to the hinge decoration on doors.

One other innovation was to appear on the ironwork of doors. In the later Middle Ages a technique known as the locksmith style introduced more intricate work on the lock plates, or *escutcheons*, and ring handles. The style is also well displayed in contemporary keys, many of which remain in use in parish churches. However, the Reformation in the sixteenth century had a radical effect on the quantity and style of church building in England and Wales, including the ironwork on doors. Medieval-style ironwork did survive in a more or less traditional form on some later doors, as at the little church of Low Ham (Somerset) built in 1625, but iron had ceased to be anything other than decorative.

Railings, screens and interior fittings

The first freestanding iron structures were screens and railings, used from the early medieval period to enclose shrines, tombs and sanctuaries. Such barriers were either liturgically desirable, as in chapel screens, or a practical necessity to protect items from pilgrims or thieves. In Britain, rood screens separating nave and chancel were usually of wood, but wrought iron was occasionally used to screen off private chapels or as railings around tombs. During the late medieval period and continuing into the seventeenth century, railings around tombs were erected for artistic effect and as a status symbol. They had ceased to be physical barriers.

The earliest, most notable examples of screens and railings were grilles protecting the tombs of important people. The grilles around the tomb of Queen Eleanor of Castile (died 1290) at Westminster Abbey and the tomb of the Black Prince (died 1376) at Canterbury Cathedral are among the best examples of this genre, which required different techniques to the hinge work on doors. The earliest grilles were composed primarily of vertical bars with scrolled lengths of iron between them, like the grille at the shrine of St Swithun in Winchester Cathedral. Towards the end of the thirteenth century the technique of stamped ornament was introduced. Above the tomb of Queen Eleanor, wife of Edward I, at Westminster Abbey, an iron grille was erected by Thomas of Leighton in 1294-5. It was intended to prevent pilgrims climbing over the tomb to reach the shrine of Edward the Confessor, England's patron saint until the fourteenth century.

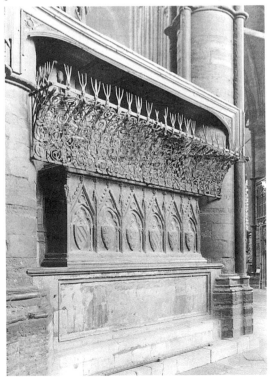

Westminster Abbey, London. The iron grille made by Thomas of Leighton in 1294-5 for the tomb of Eleanor of Castile.

11

Vertical railings came in three basic forms: in section, the bars were square, round or, from the sixteenth century, twisted in a style often known as barley twist. Above the horizontal top rail the vertical railings would terminate in *finials*. The finial was first introduced as a deterrent – the Eleanor grille has trident spikes – but subsequently became a device for terminating a railing in an aesthetically satisfying manner. The two most common forms were the spike and the fleur-de-lis, which consisted of three feathers, a popular motif in medieval art and one that was well suited to the two-dimensional effect that the smith required. Three-dimensional forms, made by welding separate pieces together, appeared from the late medieval period.

The locksmith style was invented in Italy in the thirteenth century. One of its earliest uses in England was at Canterbury Cathedral in the early fourteenth century for a choir screen. It was used probably a little later for a screen at St Albans Abbey (Hertfordshire). Both of these examples exhibit a strong Islamic flavour to their designs. As its name suggests, the style developed from the intricate work required in making locks but is best represented in larger-scale works. Previously all ironwork had been produced at the anvil when the iron was at welding heat. The locksmith style was cold work, produced at a bench in the same manner as a hard wood would be carved: by cutting, sawing, filing or drilling. Similarly, major components were fitted with mortise and tenon joints, while latticework was held together by rivets. It soon, however, became a technique used in conjunction with hot work. In place of stylised foliage, more architectural forms now became possible. The smith who made the Henry V chantry

Stanton Harcourt, Oxfordshire. A good example of early fleur-de-lis finials, of c.1400. Note the unevenness of the work.

Above left: *Cirencester, Gloucestershire. The late medieval gates to the porch are a good example of the combination of twisted and shaped bars, and fleur-de-lis and spike finials.*

Above right: *Twisted bars, scrollwork and finials to the Jennings tomb at Curry Rivel, Somerset, made c.1630.*

Right: *The locksmith, from a medieval German book of trades. Apart from the hearth in the background and the anvil in the foreground, the smith works the iron cold at a bench.*

chapel screen at Westminster Abbey in 1431 worked diagonal bars into a quatrefoil pattern below Perpendicular tracery, and at St George's Chapel in Windsor Castle John Tresilian made a screen with gates and flanking towers for the tomb of Edward IV (died 1483) in the contemporary Perpendicular style.

After the Reformation tomb railings became the predominant form of ecclesiastical ironwork. Other minor forms also emerged in the seventeenth and eighteenth centuries, such as chandelier rods and hourglass stands. A new class of structure was stands for ceremonial paraphernalia, such as maces and other mayoral insignia, and swords. Most churches in large towns such

St George's Chapel, Windsor Castle. The tomb of Edward IV (died 1483) is a tour de force of the locksmith style, designed in an architectural idiom.

as London, Bristol and Norwich contained sword rests. However, at the end of the seventeenth century a revival of wrought ironwork was primarily a secular phenomenon.

Secular uses of ironwork had been developing throughout the seventeenth century. One of the earliest iron staircase balustrades was designed c.1637 by Inigo Jones for the Queen's House in Greenwich. Iron was equally suitable for balustrades and balconies. Exterior ironwork, usually painted grey or white, or gilded, became an important component in the architectural setting of houses and gardens as wrought-iron gate screens were ideal for enclosing forecourts and formal gardens. In some of the earliest gates, as at Groombridge Place (Kent), iron was used in conjunction with wood, but all-iron railings and gates had become established by the end of the seventeenth century and were to become the dominant medium of the early eighteenth century.

Far left: *Axbridge, Somerset. Wrought-iron chandelier rods, here in the form of a crucifix, were widely used in post-Reformation churches. This eighteenth-century example was influenced by secular Baroque ironwork.*

Left: *St Stephen, Bristol. A sword rest made in the early eighteenth century, probably by William Edney. Many urban churches have similar rests for ceremonial objects.*

A detail of Jean Tijou's screen at the Privy Garden, Hampton Court Palace, Middlesex. The cresting, showing a mask, cloth of estate, eagles and foliage, is the supreme example of the repoussé technique in Britain.

Screens, gates and railings: the early eighteenth century

Jean Tijou was a Protestant master smith who came to England *c*.1685 as a refugee from his native France. Four years later he was working for the ultimate Protestant patrons – William and Mary – for whom he made iron screens for the gardens at Hampton Court (Middlesex). Until this period British smiths had never entirely shrugged off the Gothic style. Tijou was responsible for introducing a Baroque style of ironwork into England which flourished in the early eighteenth century, generally regarded as the golden age of British wrought ironwork. In 1693 he published *A New Book of Drawings Invented and Designed by Jean Tijou*, in which his style was set out. There has been much speculation as to whether any of his British followers had ever been apprenticed to Tijou, given that they were followers of a style that required mastery of a new technique, but it is also likely that Tijou's influence was disseminated by means of his pattern book.

The Baroque style depended upon a composition of leaves and flowers wrought from sheet iron, providing a solid element to contrast with routine scrollwork, and

The Privy Garden, Hampton Court Palace, Middlesex. The repoussé mask was a characteristic Tijou motif.

15

Hampton Court Palace, Middlesex. Tijou's gateway to the Great Fountain Garden, where railings and gates are used to enclose the semicircular formal garden.

composed in an ordered, symmetrical fashion. The use of sheet iron was a major innovation and required the hammering of a pattern in relief on to the sheet, known as *repoussé* work, or embossing. The sheet was prepared by drawing the design on to its back surface. This was then embedded face down on to an asphalt block and hammered cold on the reverse side to raise the ornament, giving the rough shape of the work. Next the design was turned over and the background was hammered back. The design would then be finished by applying chased ornament, sharpening up the detail.

In his screens at Hampton Court Tijou introduced several new repoussé motifs that would become standard in subsequent years, such as animal and eagle heads, facial masks, leaves and flowers. The Hampton Court screens cost £2160 for the iron and workmanship, an enormous sum for the time. He also produced balustrades for the stairs inside the house. The work was undertaken at his workshop on Hampton Court Green. His other work included: a gate screen for Cholmondeley Hall (Cheshire), for which he was paid £100 in 1695; screens in St Paul's Cathedral (London), arguably his finest work and where his repoussé urn finials can be seen; work at Chatsworth (Derbyshire) for

Jean Tijou's gates at the Clarendon Building in Oxford are one of his richest compositions.

16

The communion rail at Weston Park church, Staffordshire, of the early eighteenth century. Elaborate ecclesiastical work of the period was often, as here, due to a wealthy benefactor.

the Duke of Devonshire, although the extent of his involvement there is uncertain; and gates at Burghley House (Lincolnshire) that are similar to his gates at the Clarendon Building, Oxford. Tijou's methods were already widely used in the rest of Europe. He is credited with introducing the style to Britain and nobody was to produce work of equal lavishness. His name features regularly in contemporary documents until 1711–12, when it suddenly disappears, suggesting either his death, retirement or return to France: we do not know which.

Wrought ironwork could not have flourished as it did without new opportunities being presented by contemporary architecture. For example, Tijou's work at Hampton Court and St Paul's Cathedral was undertaken in the context of Christopher Wren's architectural designs, while John Vanbrugh's Castle Howard (North Yorkshire) and Grimsthorpe Castle (Lincolnshire) both incorporated gate screens in the setting of the house. Commissions during this period were predominantly secular. However, wrought iron was still made for churches, notably for estate churches such as Staunton Harold (Leicestershire) and Weston Park (Staffordshire). Here, too, the fashion was to use ironwork to replace the earlier fashion for wooden screens. Screens and gates, which had hitherto been confined largely to the inside of churches, were also now placed outside.

The gate screen is the characteristic form of the period and was designed following established architectural principles. Main gates were flanked by *piers* (in imitation

Trinity College, Cambridge. William Marshall's gate screen is typical in its composition: the main double gates, wide enough for a carriage, are flanked by piers, narrower pedestrian side gates and then railings. The gates have dog bars at the bottom, an ornate lock rail, and above the main gates is an elaborate overthrow.

17

Chatsworth House, Derbyshire. The gates, attributed to Richard Oddy and dated c.1720, demonstrate the use of scrolled bars to fill panels, with a minimum use of repoussé work.

of stone piers), which were either in two dimensions and flat or were square but hollow in the centre. Main double gates could be flanked by narrower pedestrian gates, which were themselves flanked by railings. Gates and railings were typically constructed with closely spaced short railings near ground level, known as *dog bars*, and were divided horizontally by the self-explanatory *lock rail*. All railings terminated in finials. Above the gates proper was elaborate cresting known as an *overthrow*, which became the ideal place to display a coat of arms.

In practice a good deal of variation is to be found in the treatment of the various components of a gate screen. Tijou and other master smiths divided their gates,

especially the lock rails and piers, into panels in which a variety of geometrical decorations were incorporated. Apart from scrolls, fretwork was introduced, utilising straight bars often intersecting to form diamond patterns. In addition to the standard repoussé motifs of animal and eagle heads, facial masks, leaves and flowers, scallop shells and coats of arms were also popular.

Within this repertoire there was scope for the development of personal style. It is from this period that smiths are usually known by name. John Gardom probably worked as an assistant to Tijou at Chatsworth (Derbyshire). Between 1705 and 1709 he made several pairs of gates at Castle Howard (North Yorkshire). The surviving gates at Chatsworth, meanwhile, are the work of Richard Oddy. The most illustrious of the Midlands smiths, however, was Robert Bakewell (1685–1752). Bakewell's first commission, begun in

Chatsworth House, Derbyshire. The gates were moved to their present position in 1829 and have two-dimensional piers with elaborate repoussé work.

18

Above: *The wrought-iron balustrade was made popular in Britain by Jean Tijou. This example was made for Melbourne Hall by Robert Bakewell in the first decade of the eighteenth century.*

Left: *Melbourne Hall, Derbyshire. The arbour at Melbourne Hall was erected by Robert Bakewell over the period 1707–11 and is a masterpiece of design and craftsmanship. It is one of Bakewell's earliest works, for which he eventually received £120. See also page 3.*

1707, is his most famous – an arbour at Melbourne Hall (Derbyshire). A masterpiece and a highly original work of garden architecture, it took four years to complete and involved modifying Tijou's repoussé work to create a more individual style. Masks and foliage were employed more sparely than they had been by Tijou and, indeed, in Bakewell's work they are subordinated to what is essentially a linear style. A reduction in the amount of repoussé work made his works less expensive to produce and he developed the wave bar to infill panels as a decorative as well as an economical device. Bakewell made his name at Melbourne and subsequently established a workshop in Derby, from where he attracted numerous commissions. His most extensive commission was for internal and external ironwork at Okeover Hall (Staffordshire), completed after his death by his assistant Benjamin Yates. Bakewell's gates at Wingerworth Hall (Derbyshire) were later moved to Penshurst Place (Kent). He also made screens for All Saints' Church, Derby, now the cathedral.

The pre-eminent smith in western Britain during this period was Robert Davies from Croes Foel near Wrexham. Biographical details of Davies are obscure

The panel flanking the main gates of the gate screen at Chirk Castle, Wrexham. The gates were made by Robert Davies in 1719.

The White Gates at Leeswood Hall, Flintshire, form one of the most impressive screens of the eighteenth century, and were made for Sir George Wynne in 1726 by Robert Davies.

Gates at Eaton Hall, Cheshire, have long been attributed to the Davies brothers. They were made c.1740. The circular motif was also used at Newnham Paddox in Leicestershire.

but he made his name by erecting gates at Chirk Castle (Wrexham) in 1719. He also worked with his younger brother John, for which reason his work is usually attributed to the 'Davies brothers'. The Davies style at Chirk was clearly derived from Tijou with its use of eagle's heads, masks and panels with embossed foliage, even if its flowing curves are not as luxurious as Tijou's work. The gate piers at Chirk are partly of cast iron, with lead wolves on the capitals, one of the earliest instances of combining wrought and cast iron. Davies subsequently made gates for a number of churches in north-east Wales and neighbouring English counties, where he developed a more economical style by the use of wave and twisted bars in panels in place of repoussé work. His other principal work was made in 1726 at Leeswood Hall (Flintshire) for Sir George Wynne. Wynne commissioned two pairs of gates, known as the White and Black Gates for the colours they were painted in, as landscape features, although their present contexts are somewhat altered from the original now that the

lodges have been taken down and the Black Gates have been moved. The White Gates lack the intricate detail of the Chirk Castle gates but they are a component of a larger-scale design.

On the border with South Wales the pre-eminent smith

The overthrow of the gates at Erddig, Wrexham. The gates have been moved on several occasions. Attributed to the Davies brothers, the chief characteristic of the ironwork is the light filigree effect of the scrollwork.

was William Edney, who worked with his brother Simon, the latter having continued the business after William's death in 1725. The Edney style has a limited hinterland, but Bristol was a natural centre for a master smith, being an affluent port city close to the ironworks of the Forest of Dean.

Oxford and Cambridge colleges commissioned a number of works in this period. In Oxford, Thomas Robinson was the predominant creative force, a smith who had worked at St Paul's Cathedral in the late seventeenth century and may therefore have been an apprentice of Tijou. About John Warren, who made gates for Clare College, Cambridge, comparatively little is known, although work at Powis Castle (Powys) has been attributed to him and he may have been related to the Thomas Warren who worked at Blenheim Palace (Oxfordshire).

The high summer of secular ironworking was soon over. During the second half of the eighteenth century there was a change in approach to the setting of country

Tewkesbury Abbey, Gloucestershire. The overthrow of the gates, made by William Edney, in which fish sprout foliage.

Trinity College, Oxford. There are many notable examples of Baroque ironwork in Oxford. The Trinity College gates are attributed to Thomas Robinson, who also designed gates for New College, and were erected in 1713.

houses. 'Capability' Brown, Humphry Repton and others introduced landscape gardens where structures such as gate screens and the formal spaces they defined were out of step with the contemporary imagination. During this period some wrought-iron gate screens were even taken down to create landscape gardens, including Tijou's gate screen at Wimpole Park (Cambridgeshire).

In addition, changes in the architectural profession led to architects gaining more individual control over craftsmen such as smiths. The consequences of this were twofold: first, there was little scope for blacksmiths to develop their own individual styles, as architects provided the designs, and secondly, in the search for economy cast iron became increasingly popular. Robert Adam, the leading Neo-Classical architect of the late eighteenth century, commissioned some wrought ironwork to his own designs but otherwise favoured cast iron (Robert Adam's brother John was a partner in the Carron Ironworks, a pioneer in architectural cast iron). Cast iron became cheaper in the latter half of the eighteenth century because of increased output consequent upon smelting with coke instead of charcoal, and the development of sand moulding that allowed intricate and complex shapes to be cast. Cast iron was now able to ape the designs of wrought iron, albeit with reduced subtlety and originality, but at a greatly reduced price.

Street furniture

The legacy of the early eighteenth century continued for a while in minor architectural forms where the Neo-Classical style was to predominate. Ironwork became part of the street scene in this period, especially in affluent towns. Robert Bakewell, for example, was commissioned in 1747 to produce ironwork for the outer arcades of the Radcliffe Camera in Oxford. Wrought-iron railings and gates were erected in front of town houses. In 1799 a Swiss visitor commented upon the 'dull, clumsy appearance' of these defensive-looking constructions and that 'the English have indeed more reasons than one for calling their houses their castles'. The railings of Georgian town houses were also likely to bear wrought-iron lamp holders: oil lamps were fitted into the tops of the holders and were lit with torches until gas lamps superseded them in the nineteenth century.

Wrought-iron gates in St Giles, Oxford. Such gates, with their flanking railings, became a common feature of towns in the eighteenth century. The gas lamp here is a later addition.

Cannock Chase Technical College, Staffordshire. These gates are typical of the simpler gates that appeared in English towns in the early eighteenth century in the wake of the more illustrious works at large country houses. Using a minimum of repoussé work, they are constructed almost entirely of bars.

The eighteenth-century railings and lamp holders at the Royal Fort House in Bristol (now part of Bristol University) are a rare survival of eighteenth-century street furniture.

Wrought-iron lamp holders from a nineteenth-century pattern book.

24

The late-seventeenth-century balcony at Wallingford Town Hall, Oxfordshire. Ironwork was particularly suited to balconies because of its comparative lightness.

The other major fashionable embellishment of houses was the balcony. Iron was well suited to balconies because of its comparative lightness. Of Venetian origin, balconies appeared in Britain in the seventeenth century. Jean Tijou produced designs for them in his *New Book of Drawings* and probably influenced the ensuing vogue for them. In the eighteenth century, small balconies featured regularly in Georgian town houses in such places as London, Bath and Cheltenham.

Neo-Classical wrought iron on the balconies of houses in the spa town of Cheltenham, Gloucestershire.

The bracket for an eighteenth-century signboard at Mere in Wiltshire. The bracket, richly provided with scrollwork, was intended to project as far as possible into the street.

Trade signs were a familiar feature of British streets until the nineteenth century. Before the introduction of house numbers and street signs they could also be found on some private houses. Wrought iron was used for such signs from the seventeenth century. Usually an iron bracket was fixed to the wall, from which the sign could be hung. Some of these signs were in sheet metal or wood. In an age of mass illiteracy they tended to be pictorial rather than textual.

The sign brackets could be quite elaborate – as advertisements they needed to stand out against the competition. The brackets often had exuberant scrolls and tended to become unstable in their attachment to the wall. In 1718 four people were killed in London by falling trade signs and legislation was introduced to curb their size. Trade signs remained a ubiquitous feature of the street scene until the nineteenth century, but a few have survived to the present day.

Gothic Revival to Post-Modern

In the nineteenth century, forges were no longer operated by independent master smiths but by firms employing waged labour. Wrought iron in this period was more commonly used in a structural context, such as the broad canopies over railway stations, the most notable example of which is the roof of St Pancras station, London, made by the Butterley Company. Nevertheless, craftsmen enjoyed a qualified revival during the nineteenth century, when leading architects turned away from factory-produced architectural embellishments towards hand-crafted decoration based on medieval traditions.

One of the first architects to exhort contemporaries to radically rethink their approach to craftsmanship was A. W. N. Pugin, the Roman Catholic church builder and pioneer of the Gothic Revival. Although Pugin produced some designs for wrought iron in his *Designs for Iron and Brass Work,* published in 1836, he was generally biased towards non-ferrous metalwork. But his influence was to be profound and to extend to the Arts and Crafts Movement of the early twentieth century.

Where decorative wrought ironwork was revived in the nineteenth century, it was often used in conjunction with cast iron and other metals. At the International Exhibition of 1862 a cast- and wrought-iron gate screen, now at Sandringham

The Sandringham Gates, as illustrated in the Catalogue of the 1862 International Exhibition. Unlike during the eighteenth century, the component rods and bars were supplied from rolling mills that gave a more perfect finish than was possible when iron bars were formed under the hammer.

Studley Royal Chapel, North Yorkshire, was designed by William Burges and completed in 1878. The use of the C-scroll is a typical reference to the early Middle Ages, while the tree motif symbolises the fecundity of nature, a favourite theme of its designer.

(Norfolk), was exhibited by the Norwich firm of Barnard, Bishop & Barnard. Significantly, the work was manufactured by the firm to the designs of the architect Thomas Jekyll. Another architect, Sir Gilbert Scott, was to enjoy a similarly fruitful partnership with the firm of Skidmore & Co in Coventry, whose works operated between 1857 and 1872. They collaborated on ironwork for nearly three hundred churches and cathedrals. Their most celebrated work was a chancel screen designed for Hereford Cathedral and made in 1862 to be displayed at the International Exhibition of that year. A combination of iron, brass, mosaic and paint, the screen is a richly

Norton sub Hamdon, Somerset. The chancel screen and pulpit have wrought ironwork designed by Henry Wilson in the Arts and Crafts style.

At the Glasgow School of Art, built 1897–9, Charles Rennie Mackintosh abandoned the tradition of the scroll in wrought iron. His stylised leaves and shields above the railings are typical Mackintosh motifs.

conceived monument to High Gothic taste. (At the time of writing the screen, given to the Victoria and Albert Museum in 1984, is awaiting restoration.)

More original reinterpretations of the Middle Ages came later in the century. William Burges designed two churches in North Yorkshire – at Skelton and Studley Royal – where his expression is typically effusive. In marked contrast is the more abstract work of G. E. Street evident in his railings at the Law Courts, London, designed in 1866 and executed a decade later by Potter of London.

Wrought iron found more favour with the advent of the Arts and Crafts Movement, of which Street's railings were a precursor. Stimulated by the work of William Morris and others, the movement encouraged craftsmen to adopt a style in which traditional elements were retained but the features of the decoration were not a self-conscious copy of historical motifs. One of the branches of the movement in Britain was Art Nouveau, developed in Belgium and France (the best-known examples of Art Nouveau ironwork are the signs for the Paris Metro designed by Hector Guimard). In Britain its most innovative exponent was Charles Rennie Mackintosh. Mackintosh used wrought iron for railings and external brackets at the Glasgow School of Art, which he designed, and for panels and signs at the nearby Willow Tea Rooms. He also included wrought-iron gates in architectural commissions such as Scotland Street School in Glasgow and Hill House in Helensburgh, near Glasgow. The work was executed by the firms of George Adam & Son and Smith & Co and was completed in the period 1897–1909. Neo-Georgian designs based on scrollwork were still in demand, however; one of the style's most notable exponents was John Seymour Lindsay. Lindsay produced ironwork for architects like Herbert Baker and Edwin Lutyens, including ironwork for the Government buildings in New Delhi.

The functional straight lines of modern architecture were not conducive to decorative ironwork, which suffered a decline in the mid twentieth century. During this period wrought iron ceased to be made, smiths now using malleable mild steel. It is in the Post-Modern period, when exponents of the applied arts have re-established their creative independence, and where the emphasis is on individuality, the quirky and humorous, that a sustained revival of the art is most likely to be seen.

Places to visit

A large quantity of decorative wrought iron has survived *in situ*, but the largest single collection is held at the Victoria and Albert Museum in London. The list below describes ironwork in places open to the public and readers are advised to enquire about opening times. The list does not include private houses, but it does include ironwork that can be viewed from public places.

Medieval ironwork is almost exclusively found in ecclesiastical buildings and most of it is on doors. The most important Norman pictorial doors are at Staplehurst (Kent), Worfield (Shropshire) and Stillingfleet (North Yorkshire). For ironwork from the thirteenth century onwards there are some good geographical clusters, perhaps the best example being the doors with die-stamped ironwork in Bedfordshire at Leighton Buzzard, Eaton Bray and Turvey.

Other doors with medieval decorative ironwork are at: Bisham, Compton, Stanford Dingley, St George's Chapel in Windsor Castle (Berkshire); Covington, Peterborough Cathedral (Cambridgeshire); Dartmouth (Devon); Durham Cathedral (County Durham); Eastwood, Elmstead, Willingale (Essex); Gloucester Cathedral, Stoke Orchard (Gloucestershire); Abbey Dore, Peterchurch (Herefordshire); Little Hormead (Hertfordshire); Barfreston, Erith, Hartley (Kent); St Margaret in Leicester (Leicestershire); Caistor, Hough-on-the-Hill, Lincoln Cathedral, Sempringham, Spalding (Lincolnshire); Haddiscoe, Raveningham, Runhall (Norfolk); Southwell Minster (Nottinghamshire); Buckland, Burford, Cuddesdon, Faringdon, Kingston Lisle, Merton College in Oxford, Sparsholt, Uffington, Westcott Barton (Oxfordshire); Edstaston, Morville (Shropshire); Meare (Somerset); Lichfield Cathedral (Staffordshire); Merton, Old Woking (Surrey); Chichester Cathedral (West Sussex); Earl's Croome (Worcestershire); Skipwith, York Minster chapter-house (North Yorkshire).

Good examples of ironwork on chests are to be found at Malpas (Cheshire); Bitterley (Shropshire); Icklingham and Santon (Suffolk). Related works are the aumbry doors at Chester Cathedral (Cheshire) and the cope chests in the chapter-house at York Minster (North Yorkshire).

Various lock plates and door handles have survived from the late medieval period, as at: St George's Chapel in Windsor Castle (Berkshire); St John's College Chapel and King's College Chapel in Cambridge (Cambridgeshire); Durham Cathedral (County Durham); St John in Cirencester (Gloucestershire); Filby, Irstead, Tunstead (Norfolk); Cound (Shropshire); Baltonsborough, Stogumber (Somerset); Eye (Suffolk); Chichester Cathedral (West Sussex).

Iron grilles, gates and screens from the medieval and post-Reformation period are mostly in cathedrals and larger churches: St George's Chapel in Windsor Castle (Berkshire); Ely Cathedral (Cambridgeshire); St John in Chester (Cheshire); St John in Cirencester (Gloucestershire); Winchester Cathedral (Hampshire); St Albans Cathedral (Hertfordshire); Canterbury Cathedral (Kent); Lincoln Cathedral, Snarford (Lincolnshire); Cote Bampton (Oxfordshire); Westminster Abbey (London); Arundel, Chichester Cathedral (West Sussex); Salisbury Cathedral (Wiltshire); and York Minster (North Yorkshire).

Tomb railings covering the period from the fourteenth to the seventeenth centuries are at: Bisham (Berkshire); Peterborough Cathedral, St John's College Chapel in Cambridge (Cambridgeshire); North Molton (Devon); Canterbury Cathedral (Kent); Lincoln Cathedral (Lincolnshire); Westminster Abbey, St Helen Bishopsgate (London); Paston (Norfolk); Burford, Stanton Harcourt, Thame (Oxfordshire); Bath Abbey, Curry Rivel, Farleigh Hungerford Castle Chapel, Low Ham, Wells Cathedral (Somerset); Arundel (West Sussex); Lydiard Tregoze, the de Borbach chantry at West Dean (Wiltshire); Ecclesfield (South Yorkshire); Tanfield and York Minster

(North Yorkshire).

During the seventeenth century ironwork was increasingly used in secular contexts, notably for gates at Traquair House (Peebles) and Ham House (London); for town-hall balconies at Wallingford (Oxfordshire) and Guildford (Surrey); and balustrades at the Old Town Hall, Dumfries (Dumfries and Galloway).

Jean Tijou's work is best seen in his screens at St Paul's Cathedral (London) and Hampton Court (Middlesex). Other work by him includes gates at the Clarendon Building in Oxford (Oxfordshire) and Burghley House (Lincolnshire), and staircase balustrades and balconies at Castle Howard (North Yorkshire) and Chatsworth (Derbyshire).

The work of the principal Midlands smith, Robert Bakewell, can be seen at Melbourne Hall and Derby Cathedral (Derbyshire); the church at Staunton Harold (Leicestershire); and Kirkleatham Hospital, Redcar (Yorkshire). Other work attributed to him is at Penshurst Place (Kent). John Gardom's work can be seen at Chatsworth (Derbyshire) and Castle Howard (North Yorkshire), the former also having gates attributed to Richard Oddy. There are gate screens by Thomas Robinson at New College and Trinity College in Oxford, while gates at Magdalen College are by an unknown smith. Cambridge colleges have an equal number of wrought-iron gate screens, including those at Clare College by John Warren and Trinity College by William Marshall, while the screens at the Wren Library of Trinity College are by William Partridge. William Marshall's work can also be seen in his chancel screen at St Mary in Warwick (Warwickshire).

Gates by Robert Davies are numerous. They include Chirk Castle and Erddig (Wrexham); Eaton House (Cheshire); and the White and Black Gates at Leeswood Hall (Flintshire). For local churches, his best work is the gate screen to the churchyard at St Giles in Wrexham and the communion rail inside the church, and at St Peter in Ruthin (Denbighshire), Malpas (Cheshire) and Oswestry (Shropshire). William Edney's work is best seen in his screens at St Mary Redcliffe (Bristol), Tredegar House (Newport) and gates at Tewkesbury Abbey (Gloucestershire).

Other good examples of eighteenth-century Baroque ironwork in ecclesiastical settings are: screens and gates at St Magnus and St Andrew Undershaft (London); Weston Park (Staffordshire); Birmingham Cathedral; St Mary in Warwick by Nicholas Parris (Warwickshire); and Lydiard Tregoze (Wiltshire). Other secular gate screens can be seen at: Grimsthorpe Castle by Edward Nutt and Belton House (Lincolnshire); Dulwich College (London); Blenheim Palace (Oxfordshire); and Powis Castle by John Warren (Powys).

There are many surviving examples of sword or mace rests in urban churches in London (St Helen Bishopsgate, St Magnus, St James Garlickhythe, St Andrew Undershaft) and Norwich (St George, St George Tombland, St John, St Mary at Coslany, St Michael-at-Plea, St Peter Mancroft), a mace rest by Nicholas Parris at St Mary in Warwick (Warwickshire) and a stand for mayoral insignia dated 1677 at Wilton (Wiltshire). Bristol churches have sword rests from the seventeenth century (St Philip, St Michael, St Thomas, Christchurch), the eighteenth century (St Mark, St James, St John and St Stephen) and early nineteenth century (St Paul).

Examples of wrought iron from the nineteenth and twentieth centuries can also be visited. These include G. E. Street's ironwork for the Law Courts (London) and Thomas Jekyll's gates at Sandringham (Norfolk). Screens by Scott and Skidmore are at Lichfield and Worcester Cathedrals, the former with other screens and a pulpit by Skidmore. A pulpit and screen by Henry Wilson are at Norton sub Hamdon (Somerset) and early-twentieth-century screens by P. Krall are at Kedleston (Derbyshire). Work by Charles Rennie Mackintosh can be seen in Glasgow at the School of Art, Willow Tea Rooms and the Scotland Street School Museum of Education, and at Hill House, Helensburgh (Argyll and Bute).

Further reading

Details of the ironwork described in the previous chapter can be found in *The Buildings of England* series by Nikolaus Pevsner and others, and the companion volumes for Wales and Scotland by various authors. General works covering wrought iron in more detail are:

Campbell, Marion. *Decorative Ironwork*. Victoria and Albert Museum, 1997.

Chatwin, Amina. *Cheltenham's Ornamental Ironwork*. Published by the author, second edition 1984.

Chatwin, Amina. *Into the New Iron Age: Modern British Blacksmiths*. Coach House Publishing, 1995.

Dunkerley, S. *Robert Bakewell: Artist Blacksmith*. Scarthin Books, 1988.

Edwards, Ifor. *Davies Brothers, Gatesmiths*. Welsh Arts Council, 1977.

Geddes, Jane. 'Iron', in *English Medieval Industries*, edited by Blair and Ramsay, Hambledon Press, 1993.

Geddes, Jane. *Medieval Decorative Ironwork in England*. Society of Antiquaries Research Report 59, 1999.

Harris, John. *English Decorative Ironwork from Contemporary Source Books 1610–1836*. Alec Tiranti, 1960.

Lindsay, John Seymour. *An Anatomy of English Wrought Iron*. Alec Tiranti, 1964.

Lister, Raymond. *Decorative Wrought Iron in Great Britain*. Bell & Sons, 1957.

The Swan Gates at St Hugh's College, Oxford, were designed by Laurence Whistler and made in 1986 by R. Quinnell.